The New Cognitive Behavioral Therapy for Anger Management

Resolve Issues Peacefully, Defuse Triggers and Manage Difficult Emotions Using CBT Mindfulness Skills

Carson Ritchie

Table of Contents

My Journey to Anger Management Success 5

Introduction 8

Why Anger Management Matters 8

The Evolution of CBT in Anger Management 10

How This Book Can Help You 12

Part I: Understanding Anger 15

1. The Nature of Anger 16

What Is Anger? 16

Types of Anger: Understanding Your Anger Profile 18

The Physiological and Psychological Impact of Anger ... 20

2. The Cognitive-Behavioral Model of Anger 24

Exploring the ABCs of Anger: Activating Events, Beliefs, and Consequences 24

The Role of Thoughts in Anger 26

Behavioral Patterns and Triggers 28

Part II: CBT Techniques for Anger Management 30

3. Identifying and Challenging Irrational Beliefs 31

Recognizing Common Anger Triggers 31

Cognitive Restructuring: Changing Your Thought Patterns 33

Techniques for Disputing Irrational Beliefs 36

4. Behavioral Strategies for Anger Control 39

Assertiveness Training: Communicating Effectively 39

Problem-Solving Skills: Resolving Conflict Constructively 42

Relaxation Techniques: Managing Physiological Arousal 45

5. Mindfulness and Anger 48

The Role of Mindfulness in Anger Management 48

Mindfulness-Based Cognitive Therapy (MBCT) 50

Practicing Mindfulness: Exercises and Strategies 53

Part III: Applying CBT in Everyday Life 58

6. Managing Anger in Relationships 59

Communicating Assertively with Loved Ones 59

Conflict Resolution Skills for Couples 61

Building Healthy Boundaries 64

7. Anger in the Workplace 69

Dealing with Anger in Professional Settings 69

Assertive Communication with Colleagues and Supervisors 73

Stress Management Techniques for Work-Related Anger 76

8. Self-Care and Long-Term Anger Management 80

Developing a Personalized Anger Management Plan 80

Lifestyle Changes for Anger Reduction 83

Seeking Support: Therapy, Support Groups, and Online
Resources 86

Conclusion 90

Embracing a Life Free from Unnecessary Anger 90

My Journey to Anger Management Success

I'll never forget the moment when I realized I needed to make a change. It was a typical day at work, filled with deadlines, meetings, and the usual stressors that come with a demanding job. But when a colleague made a careless comment that triggered an intense wave of anger within me, I knew something had to give. My explosive reaction left me feeling ashamed and out of control, and I knew I couldn't continue down that path.

That's when I decided to pick up "The New CBT for Anger Management." I had heard about cognitive-behavioral therapy (CBT) before, but I never truly understood how it could help me manage my anger until I delved into the pages of this book.

As I worked through the exercises and techniques outlined in the book, I began to unravel the underlying patterns and beliefs that fueled my anger. I learned to identify the activating events that triggered my emotional responses, the irrational beliefs that distorted my perception of reality, and the negative consequences that resulted from my unchecked anger.

One of the most powerful tools I discovered was cognitive restructuring. By challenging my negative thought patterns and replacing them with more balanced and rational thoughts, I gained a newfound sense of control over my emotions. I also learned practical strategies for assertive communication, problem-solving, and relaxation, which helped me navigate challenging situations with greater ease and confidence.

But perhaps the most transformative aspect of my journey was the practice of mindfulness. Through mindfulness exercises and meditation practices, I learned to cultivate greater self-awareness and emotional regulation, enabling me to respond to life's triggers with calmness and clarity rather than react impulsively out of anger.

Over time, I began to notice profound changes in myself and in the way I interacted with the world around me. My relationships improved as I communicated more effectively and empathetically with others. I felt more confident in my ability to handle stress and adversity without resorting to anger as my default coping mechanism. And perhaps most importantly, I experienced a newfound sense of inner peace and contentment that I hadn't felt in years.

Today, I can proudly say that I've overcome my struggles with anger thanks to the transformative power of CBT. While I still face challenges and setbacks from time to time, I now have the tools and resilience to navigate them with grace and resilience. "The New CBT for Anger Management" not only changed my life—it gave me the keys to unlock a happier, healthier, and more fulfilling future.

If you're struggling with anger issues like I was, I urge you to give CBT a try. You might just discover, like I did, that the path to anger management success is closer than you think.

Introduction

Why Anger Management Matters

Unmanaged anger can wreak havoc on our personal and professional lives in myriad ways. From strained relationships and damaged reputations to health problems and legal consequences, the repercussions of uncontrolled anger can be far-reaching and long-lasting. Consider the following:

1. Relationships: Anger can erode trust, communication, and intimacy in our relationships. Explosive outbursts or passive-aggressive behavior can drive loved ones away and leave us feeling isolated and disconnected.

2. Physical Health: Chronic anger has been linked to a host of health problems, including high blood pressure, heart disease, weakened immune system, and even increased risk of stroke. The physiological effects of anger can take a toll on our bodies over time, leading to serious health complications.

3. Mental Health: Anger can also take a toll on our mental well-being, contributing to stress, anxiety, depression, and other mood disorders. Left unchecked, chronic anger can fuel a cycle of negative thinking and emotional distress, further exacerbating mental health issues.

4. Professional Consequences: In the workplace, uncontrolled anger can damage our professional reputation, hinder career advancement, and even lead to disciplinary action or termination. Angry outbursts or conflicts with coworkers can create a toxic work environment and undermine productivity and morale.

Breaking the Cycle of Anger

While anger itself is not inherently bad, it's how we respond to it that truly matters. The key to effective anger management lies in understanding the underlying causes of our anger and developing healthy coping strategies to express and manage it constructively. By breaking the cycle of anger, we can reclaim control over our emotions and our lives.

The Role of Cognitive-Behavioral Therapy (CBT)

Cognitive-behavioral therapy (CBT) offers a structured and evidence-based approach to anger management that addresses both the cognitive and behavioral aspects of anger. By identifying and challenging irrational beliefs, restructuring negative thought patterns, and developing practical skills for communication and conflict resolution, CBT equips individuals with the tools they need to navigate anger more effectively.

The Promise of Change

The journey to effective anger management is not always easy, but it is undoubtedly worth it. By committing to self-awareness, introspection, and growth, we can break free from the grip of unnecessary anger and cultivate greater peace, resilience, and fulfillment in our lives. In the chapters that follow, we'll explore the principles and techniques of CBT for anger management in greater detail, providing you with the knowledge and resources you need to embark on your own journey of transformation.

The Evolution of CBT in Anger Management

CBT traces its roots to the work of psychologists Aaron Beck and Albert Ellis in the 1950s and 1960s. Dissatisfied with traditional psychoanalytic approaches to therapy, Beck and Ellis pioneered a new model that focused on the interplay between thoughts, feelings, and behaviors. They posited that irrational beliefs and distorted thinking patterns contribute to emotional distress and maladaptive behavior, and that by identifying and challenging these beliefs, individuals can change their emotional responses and improve their functioning.

In the early years of CBT, anger management was not a primary focus of treatment. Instead, CBT was primarily used to treat mood disorders such as depression and anxiety. However, clinicians soon recognized the relevance of CBT principles to anger-related issues, as distorted thinking patterns and maladaptive behaviors often underlie problematic anger responses.

As interest in anger management grew, researchers and clinicians began to develop specialized CBT interventions tailored to address anger-related issues. These interventions drew upon core CBT principles such as cognitive restructuring, behavioral activation, and skills training, but were adapted to specifically target the unique cognitive and behavioral patterns associated with anger.

In recent years, there has been a growing interest in integrating mindfulness-based approaches into CBT for anger management. Mindfulness, rooted in Eastern contemplative traditions, emphasizes present-moment awareness and nonjudgmental acceptance of one's thoughts, feelings, and sensations. By cultivating mindfulness skills, individuals can develop greater self-awareness and emotional regulation, enabling them to respond to anger triggers with greater calmness and clarity.

Today, CBT remains a leading approach to anger management, with a wealth of research supporting its effectiveness in reducing anger symptoms and improving overall functioning. However, the field continues to evolve, with researchers exploring new interventions, techniques, and delivery methods to enhance the efficacy and accessibility of CBT for anger-related issues. From online interventions and smartphone apps to cultural adaptations and integrated treatment approaches, the future of CBT in anger management holds promise for continued innovation and advancement.

How This Book Can Help You

Understanding Your Anger

The first step towards effective anger management is understanding your anger—its triggers, patterns, and underlying beliefs. This book provides you with the tools and insights you need to gain a deeper understanding of your anger, empowering you to recognize the thoughts, feelings, and behaviors that contribute to your anger responses.

Learning Cognitive-Behavioral Techniques

Central to this book is the exploration of cognitive-behavioral therapy (CBT) techniques for managing anger. You'll learn practical strategies for identifying and challenging irrational beliefs, restructuring negative thought patterns, and developing healthier coping mechanisms for dealing with anger triggers. These techniques are grounded in empirical research and clinical evidence, ensuring their effectiveness in helping you manage your anger more effectively.

Practical Exercises and Activities

Throughout the book, you'll find a variety of practical exercises and activities designed to help you apply CBT techniques to your own life. From journaling prompts and thought records to role-playing scenarios and relaxation exercises, these activities provide you with hands-on tools for implementing the strategies outlined in each chapter. By actively engaging with the material, you'll deepen your understanding of anger management concepts and enhance your ability to apply them in real-world situations.

Addressing Common Challenges

Anger management is not always easy, and this book acknowledges the challenges you may encounter along the way. Whether it's dealing with setbacks and relapses, navigating difficult relationships, or managing anger in the workplace, you'll find practical guidance and strategies for overcoming common obstacles and staying on track towards your goals.

Promoting Long-Term Change

Ultimately, this book is about promoting long-term change and empowering you to live a life free from the grip of unnecessary anger. By providing you with the knowledge, skills, and support you need to manage your anger more effectively, it lays the foundation for lasting transformation and greater emotional well-being. Whether you're struggling with explosive outbursts of rage or simmering resentment beneath the surface, this book offers hope, guidance, and a path forward towards a brighter future.

Part I: Understanding Anger

1. The Nature of Anger

What Is Anger?

Anger is a complex and multifaceted emotion that manifests in response to perceived threats, injustices, or frustrations. It is a universal human experience, spanning cultures, ages, and genders, and it serves a variety of adaptive functions.

Understanding the Emotional Experience of Anger

At its core, anger is characterized by a state of heightened arousal and activation, accompanied by feelings of irritation, hostility, and agitation. It is often triggered by events or circumstances that are perceived as unjust, threatening, or frustrating, and it can vary in intensity from mild annoyance to intense rage.

The Function of Anger

While anger is often associated with negative connotations, it serves several important functions in human behavior:

1. Self-Protection: Anger can serve as a self-protective mechanism, signaling to others that our boundaries have been violated or that we are facing a perceived threat. It can mobilize us to take action to defend ourselves or assert our rights.

2. Social Signaling: Anger communicates important information to others about our emotional state and our boundaries. It can signal dissatisfaction with a situation or behavior, assert dominance or authority, and establish social hierarchies.

3. Motivational Force: Anger can serve as a powerful motivational force, energizing us to address injustices, overcome obstacles, and pursue our goals. It can fuel activism, advocacy, and social change.

The Physiological Response to Anger

Anger is accompanied by a distinct physiological response that prepares the body to respond to perceived threats. This response, often referred to as the "fight or flight" response, is characterized by increased heart rate, elevated blood pressure, heightened muscle tension, and the release of stress hormones such as adrenaline and cortisol.

The Cognitive Component of Anger

In addition to its emotional and physiological aspects, anger also has a cognitive component that involves the interpretation and appraisal of events. Our thoughts, beliefs, and interpretations play a crucial role in shaping our experience of anger, influencing the intensity of our emotional response and the way we express and manage our anger.

Types of Anger: Understanding Your Anger Profile

Anger is a multifaceted emotion that can manifest in various ways, and understanding the different types of anger can provide valuable insight into your own anger profile.

Reactive Anger

Reactive anger is perhaps the most recognizable type of anger. It occurs in response to a perceived threat, injustice, or provocation, and it is often accompanied by an immediate and intense emotional reaction. Reactive anger tends to be impulsive and uncontrolled, leading to behaviors such as yelling, shouting, or physical aggression. Individuals who experience reactive anger may struggle to regulate their emotions in the heat of the moment and may later regret their actions.

Passive Aggressive Anger

Passive aggressive anger involves expressing anger indirectly or covertly, often through subtle forms of defiance, resistance, or sabotage. Instead of confronting the source of their anger directly, individuals may engage in behaviors such as sarcasm, procrastination, or withholding communication as a way of expressing their displeasure. Passive aggressive anger can be difficult to identify and address, as it is often masked by superficial compliance or avoidance.

Suppressed Anger

Suppressed anger occurs when individuals consciously or unconsciously suppress or deny their feelings of anger. Instead of expressing their anger outwardly, they may internalize it, leading to feelings of resentment, bitterness, or hostility. Suppressed anger can manifest in physical symptoms such as headaches, digestive issues, or insomnia, and it can have long-term consequences for both physical and mental health.

Chronic Anger

Chronic anger refers to a persistent and pervasive pattern of anger that extends over time. Unlike reactive anger, which is triggered by specific events or situations, chronic anger may become a habitual response to life's stressors. Individuals who experience chronic anger may perceive the world as hostile or unfair, leading to a constant state of irritability, frustration, or cynicism. Chronic anger can have serious implications for health and well-being, contributing to problems such as high blood pressure, heart disease, and depression.

Constructive Anger

Contrary to popular belief, not all forms of anger are destructive or unhealthy. Constructive anger involves channeling feelings of anger into productive and adaptive behaviors, such as assertiveness, problem-solving, or advocacy. Instead of lashing out impulsively or suppressing their anger, individuals who experience constructive anger use it as a catalyst for positive change and growth. Constructive anger can lead to improved communication, strengthened relationships, and greater personal empowerment.

The Physiological and Psychological Impact of Anger

Anger is not merely an emotional experience; it also has profound effects on both our physiological and psychological well-being.

Physiological Impact

Anger triggers a cascade of physiological responses in the body, preparing us to respond to perceived threats or challenges. This physiological arousal, often referred to as the "fight or flight" response, is characterized by the release of stress hormones such as adrenaline and cortisol, increased heart rate, elevated blood pressure, and heightened muscle tension.

While these physiological changes are adaptive in the short term, helping us to mobilize our resources and respond to immediate threats, chronic or uncontrolled anger can have serious implications for our physical health. Prolonged activation of the stress response can contribute to a variety of health problems, including:

- Cardiovascular Issues: Chronic anger has been linked to an increased risk of heart disease, hypertension, and stroke. The constant strain on the cardiovascular system can lead to damage to blood vessels, inflammation, and other risk factors for heart problems.
- Weakened Immune System: Prolonged stress and anger can suppress the immune system, making us more susceptible to infections, illnesses, and autoimmune disorders. Chronic inflammation associated with anger can exacerbate existing health conditions and slow down the body's healing processes.

- Digestive Disorders: Anger can also impact the digestive system, leading to problems such as irritable bowel syndrome (IBS), acid reflux, and stomach ulcers. Stress and tension associated with anger can disrupt normal digestion and exacerbate gastrointestinal symptoms.

Psychological Impact

In addition to its physiological effects, anger can also take a toll on our psychological well-being, influencing our thoughts, emotions, and behaviors in profound ways. Chronic or unmanaged anger has been linked to a variety of psychological issues, including:

- Stress and Anxiety: Anger and stress are closely interconnected, with chronic anger contributing to heightened levels of stress and anxiety. The constant activation of the stress response can lead to feelings of overwhelm, tension, and nervousness, making it difficult to relax and unwind.

- Depression: While anger is often associated with outward expressions of emotion, it can also be turned inward, leading to feelings of sadness, hopelessness, and despair. Chronic anger can contribute to the development or exacerbation of depressive symptoms, making it harder to find joy or satisfaction in life.

- Interpersonal Problems: Uncontrolled anger can strain relationships with family members, friends, and colleagues, leading to conflicts, misunderstandings, and social isolation. Anger may drive others away, leaving individuals feeling lonely, rejected, or misunderstood.

2. The Cognitive-Behavioral Model of Anger

Exploring the ABCs of Anger: Activating Events, Beliefs, and Consequences

The cognitive-behavioral model of anger provides a framework for understanding how our thoughts, beliefs, and behaviors contribute to the experience and expression of anger.

Activating Events

Activating events are the external triggers or stimuli that set off the anger response. These events can vary widely and may include anything from a perceived slight or injustice to a frustrating setback or disappointment. Activating events can be real or perceived, objective or subjective, but they all have the potential to elicit an emotional reaction.

For example, imagine you're stuck in traffic on your way to an important meeting. The traffic jam is the activating event that triggers feelings of frustration and irritation. Similarly, receiving criticism from a colleague or experiencing a personal setback can serve as activating events that provoke anger.

Beliefs

Beliefs refer to the thoughts, interpretations, and assumptions we hold about ourselves, others, and the world around us. These beliefs play a crucial role in shaping our emotional responses to activating events. In the context of anger, beliefs are often irrational or distorted, leading to exaggerated or disproportionate reactions.

For instance, if you believe that you must always be in control and that any disruption to your plans is unacceptable, you may react with anger when faced with unexpected obstacles or delays. Similarly, if you hold rigid beliefs about fairness or justice and perceive any deviation from these standards as a personal affront, you may respond with anger towards perceived injustices.

Consequences

Consequences refer to the outcomes or results of our emotional responses to activating events. These consequences can be both internal and external, affecting our thoughts, emotions, and behaviors as well as our relationships and interactions with others.

For example, responding to a traffic jam with anger may lead to increased stress, tension, and frustration, as well as potential conflicts with other drivers. Similarly, expressing anger towards a colleague may damage your professional relationship and undermine teamwork and collaboration.

The Interaction of the ABCs

The cognitive-behavioral model suggests that it is not the activating events themselves that directly cause our emotional responses, but rather the way we interpret and appraise these events. Our beliefs and interpretations shape our emotional reactions, which in turn influence our behavioral responses and the consequences that follow.

The Role of Thoughts in Anger

In the cognitive-behavioral model of anger, thoughts play a central role in shaping our emotional experiences and behavioral responses.

Cognitive Appraisal Theory

According to cognitive appraisal theory, our emotions are not solely determined by external events, but rather by the way we interpret and appraise those events. When we encounter a situation that triggers anger, we engage in a process of cognitive appraisal, evaluating the situation based on our beliefs, expectations, and past experiences.

For example, if someone cuts you off in traffic, your initial reaction may be one of anger. However, the intensity of your anger will depend on how you interpret the situation. If you believe that the driver intentionally cut you off out of malice, your anger may be more intense than if you interpret the action as an innocent mistake.

Cognitive Distortions

Cognitive distortions are irrational or exaggerated thought patterns that contribute to the experience of anger. These distortions often involve errors in reasoning or faulty interpretations of events, leading to negative emotions such as anger, frustration, or resentment.

Common cognitive distortions associated with anger include:

- All-or-nothing thinking: Seeing things in black-and-white terms, with no room for shades of gray. For example, believing that if you're not perfect, you're a complete failure.

- Catastrophizing: Assuming the worst possible outcome will occur. For example, thinking that a minor inconvenience is a catastrophe.

- Mind-reading: Assuming you know what others are thinking or intending without any evidence. For example, believing that someone is deliberately trying to upset you without considering alternative explanations.

- Personalization: Taking responsibility for things that are outside of your control. For example, blaming yourself for someone else's actions or feelings.

Identifying and challenging these cognitive distortions is a key component of cognitive restructuring, a cognitive-behavioral technique used to modify maladaptive thought patterns and promote more adaptive and rational thinking.

Behavioral Patterns

In the cognitive-behavioral model of anger, behavioral patterns and triggers play a crucial role in the expression and management of anger.

Behavioral Patterns

Behavioral patterns refer to the ways in which individuals express and respond to anger. These patterns can vary widely from person to person and may include both overt and covert behaviors. Some common behavioral patterns associated with anger include:

- Aggression: Aggressive behavior involves the direct expression of anger through actions such as yelling, shouting, or physical violence. This behavior is often driven by a desire to assert dominance or control over others and can have serious consequences for relationships and well-being.

- Passive Aggression: Passive-aggressive behavior involves expressing anger indirectly or covertly, often through subtle forms of resistance or sabotage. This behavior may include sarcasm, procrastination, or withholding communication as a way of expressing displeasure while avoiding direct confrontation.

- Avoidance: Some individuals may respond to anger by avoiding or withdrawing from situations or people that trigger their anger. This behavior may provide temporary relief from feelings of anger, but it can also lead to social isolation and interpersonal conflicts if not addressed.

- Self-Harm: In some cases, individuals may direct their anger inward, engaging in self-destructive behaviors such as substance abuse, self-harm, or reckless behavior. This behavior may serve as a way of coping with overwhelming emotions or as a form of punishment for perceived failures or inadequacies.

Part II: CBT Techniques for Anger Management

3. Identifying and Challenging Irrational Beliefs

Recognizing Common Anger Triggers

Understanding the triggers that lead to anger is essential for effective anger management. By recognizing these triggers, individuals can gain insight into the underlying beliefs and thought patterns that contribute to their anger responses.

Frustration

Frustration arises when individuals encounter obstacles or challenges that prevent them from achieving their goals or desires. Common sources of frustration include:

- Traffic congestion or delays
- Technical malfunctions or equipment failures
- Long waits or delays in service
- Inefficient or uncooperative colleagues or service providers

Injustice

Perceived injustices or unfair treatment can trigger feelings of anger and resentment. Examples of situations that may provoke feelings of injustice include:

- Being treated unfairly or disrespectfully by others
- Experiencing discrimination or prejudice based on race, gender, or other characteristics
- Witnessing acts of injustice or inequality in society or the workplace

Criticism or Rejection

Criticism or rejection from others can be particularly triggering for individuals with low self-esteem or a strong need for approval. Common sources of criticism or rejection include:

- Negative feedback or criticism from supervisors, colleagues, or peers
- Rejection or exclusion from social groups or activities
- Disapproval or disappointment from friends, family members, or romantic partners

Stress

Chronic stress or overwhelming demands can lower individuals' tolerance for frustration and increase their susceptibility to anger. Sources of stress that may trigger anger include:

- Work-related stressors such as deadlines, workload, or conflicts with coworkers

- Financial difficulties, including debt, unemployment, or financial insecurity
- Relationship problems, including conflicts with romantic partners, family members, or friends

Personalization

Personalization involves attributing external events or circumstances to personal flaws or failures. This cognitive distortion can lead individuals to feel personally attacked or criticized, even when the situation is not directed at them. Common examples of personalization include:

- Taking constructive feedback as a personal attack on one's competence or worth
- Assuming that others' negative behaviors or attitudes are a reflection of one's own inadequacies
- Blaming oneself for external events or circumstances that are beyond one's control

Cognitive Restructuring: Changing Your Thought Patterns

Cognitive restructuring is a fundamental technique in cognitive-behavioral therapy (CBT) that aims to identify and challenge irrational beliefs and replace them with more rational and adaptive thoughts.

Recognizing Cognitive Distortions

The first step in cognitive restructuring is to recognize and identify cognitive distortions in your thinking. This involves becoming aware of the automatic thoughts that arise in response to triggering events and examining them for signs of irrationality or distortion. Some common cognitive distortions associated with anger include:

- Jumping to conclusions: Making assumptions or drawing conclusions without sufficient evidence.
- Overgeneralization: Drawing sweeping conclusions based on limited evidence or isolated incidents.
- Emotional reasoning: Assuming that your feelings reflect objective reality or that your emotional reactions are justified by the situation.
- Should statements: Using words like "should," "must," or "ought to" to impose unrealistic expectations on yourself or others.

Challenging Irrational Beliefs

Once you have identified cognitive distortions in your thinking, the next step is to challenge and reframe them using rational, evidence-based thinking. This involves examining the evidence for and against your beliefs, considering alternative explanations or perspectives, and generating more balanced and realistic interpretations of the situation.

Some effective strategies for challenging irrational beliefs include:

- Reality testing: Examining the evidence for and against a particular belief or interpretation of a situation.
- Decatastrophizing: Evaluating the likelihood and consequences of a feared outcome and considering more realistic alternatives.
- Alternative explanations: Generating alternative explanations or interpretations of events that are less negative or biased.
- Balanced thinking: Encouraging a more balanced and objective perspective by considering both positive and negative aspects of a situation.

Reframing Your Thoughts

Once you have challenged and modified your irrational beliefs, the final step is to reframe your thoughts in a more rational and adaptive way. This involves replacing negative or distorted thoughts with more balanced and realistic ones that are based on evidence and objective reasoning. By reframing your thoughts, you can reduce the intensity of your emotional reactions and cultivate greater emotional resilience and well-being.

Techniques for Disputing Irrational Beliefs

By applying these techniques, individuals can develop greater self-awareness, challenge distorted thinking patterns, and cultivate more balanced and rational perspectives on triggering events.

Socratic Questioning

Socratic questioning is a technique derived from the Socratic method of philosophical inquiry. It involves asking probing questions to encourage individuals to examine the validity and rationality of their beliefs. Some examples of Socratic questions that can be used to dispute irrational beliefs include:

- "What evidence supports this belief?"
- "What evidence contradicts this belief?"
- "Is there another way to interpret this situation?"
- "What would I say to a friend who had a similar belief?"

By guiding individuals through a process of self-inquiry and critical reflection, Socratic questioning can help them identify inconsistencies or flaws in their thinking and develop more rational and adaptive beliefs.

Behavioral Experiments

Behavioral experiments involve testing the validity of irrational beliefs through direct observation and experimentation. This technique encourages individuals to gather real-world evidence to evaluate the accuracy and utility of their beliefs. For example, if someone holds the irrational belief that they must always be in control to avoid feeling anxious or vulnerable, they might conduct an experiment where they intentionally relinquish control in a low-stakes situation and observe the consequences.

By engaging in behavioral experiments, individuals can challenge their irrational beliefs in a concrete and tangible way, providing opportunities for experiential learning and cognitive restructuring.

Thought Records

Thought records are a structured form of self-monitoring that involves documenting triggering events, associated thoughts and emotions, and alternative interpretations or responses. By recording their thoughts and reactions in the moment, individuals can gain insight into the cognitive processes underlying their anger and identify patterns or themes in their thinking.

Once the thoughts have been recorded, individuals can then use cognitive restructuring techniques such as reality testing, decatastrophizing, and alternative explanations to dispute irrational beliefs and reframe their perspectives on triggering events.

Role-Playing and Imagery

Role-playing and imagery techniques involve mentally rehearsing alternative responses to triggering events or challenging situations. By visualizing themselves responding in more adaptive and constructive ways, individuals can weaken the grip of irrational beliefs and develop new, more adaptive behavioral patterns.

For example, individuals can imagine themselves encountering a triggering event and responding calmly and assertively, rather than reacting with anger or aggression. Through repeated practice and visualization, individuals can strengthen their ability to respond to triggering events in a more adaptive and constructive manner.

4. Behavioral Strategies for Anger Control

Assertiveness Training: Communicating Effectively

Assertiveness is the ability to express oneself openly, honestly, and respectfully while also respecting the rights and boundaries of others. It involves communicating your thoughts, feelings, and needs directly and assertively, without resorting to passive or aggressive behaviors.

Unlike passive communication, which involves avoiding conflict and accommodating others' needs at the expense of one's own, or aggressive communication, which involves asserting one's needs at the expense of others' rights and feelings, assertive communication seeks to find a balance between expressing oneself and respecting others.

Key Principles of Assertive Communication

Assertive communication is characterized by several key principles:

- Clear and Direct Communication: Assertive individuals express themselves clearly, directly, and honestly, without beating around the bush or resorting to vague or ambiguous language.

- Respect for Boundaries: Assertive individuals respect their own boundaries and the boundaries of others, communicating their needs and preferences while also recognizing and honoring the rights and autonomy of others.

- Active Listening: Assertive communication involves actively listening to others' perspectives, feelings, and needs, and responding empathetically and non-judgmentally.

- Use of "I" Statements: Assertive individuals use "I" statements to express their thoughts, feelings, and needs, taking ownership of their experiences and avoiding blame or criticism of others.

Assertiveness Training Techniques

Assertiveness training involves a variety of techniques and exercises designed to help individuals develop and strengthen their assertive communication skills. Some common assertiveness training techniques include:

- Role-Playing: Role-playing exercises allow individuals to practice assertive communication in simulated scenarios, experimenting with different approaches and responses in a safe and supportive environment.

- Assertiveness Scripts: Assertiveness scripts provide individuals with pre-written statements or scripts that they can use to communicate assertively in specific situations, such as expressing dissatisfaction with a product or service or setting boundaries with a friend or colleague.

- Behavioral Rehearsal: Behavioral rehearsal involves mentally rehearsing assertive responses to challenging situations or interactions, visualizing oneself responding confidently and assertively.

- Feedback and Reinforcement: Providing feedback and reinforcement is an essential component of assertiveness training, helping individuals identify areas for improvement and build confidence in their assertive communication skills.

Applying Assertiveness in Anger Management

Assertiveness training is particularly useful in the context of anger management, as it empowers individuals to express their needs, thoughts, and feelings in a constructive and respectful manner. By communicating assertively, individuals can assert their boundaries, address conflicts, and resolve disagreements without resorting to passive or aggressive behaviors.

Problem-Solving Skills: Resolving Conflict Constructively

Problem-solving skills involve a systematic approach to identifying, analyzing, and resolving conflicts or challenges in a constructive and collaborative manner. This approach emphasizes communication, collaboration, and creativity in finding mutually acceptable solutions to disagreements or disputes.

Key Steps in Problem-Solving

Effective problem-solving typically involves the following key steps:

- Identifying the Problem: The first step in problem-solving is to clearly define and identify the underlying issues or concerns that are contributing to the conflict. This may involve gathering information, listening actively to others' perspectives, and clarifying expectations and goals.

- Generating Solutions: Once the problem has been identified, individuals can brainstorm and generate potential solutions or strategies for addressing the conflict. This step encourages creativity and open-mindedness, allowing individuals to explore a range of possible alternatives.

- Evaluating Solutions: After generating potential solutions, individuals evaluate each option based on its feasibility, effectiveness, and potential consequences. This involves considering the needs and preferences of all parties involved and weighing the pros and cons of each alternative.

- Implementing the Solution: Once a mutually acceptable solution has been identified, individuals work together to implement and execute the plan of action. This may involve setting specific goals, establishing timelines, and allocating resources or responsibilities as needed.

- Evaluating the Outcome: After implementing the solution, individuals evaluate the effectiveness of the intervention and its impact on the conflict. This involves reflecting on what worked well, what could be improved, and any lessons learned for future conflicts.

Communication Skills in Problem-Solving

Effective communication is essential for successful problem-solving and conflict resolution. Some key communication skills that support constructive problem-solving include:

- Active Listening: Listening actively and empathetically to others' perspectives, feelings, and needs without interrupting or judging.
- Clarification: Asking clarifying questions to ensure mutual understanding and avoid misunderstandings or misinterpretations.
- Assertion: Expressing one's thoughts, feelings, and needs assertively and respectfully, while also respecting the rights and perspectives of others.
- Negotiation: Engaging in constructive negotiation and compromise to find mutually acceptable solutions to disagreements or conflicts.

Applying Problem-Solving Skills in Anger Management

Problem-solving skills are invaluable in the context of anger management, as they provide individuals with a structured and systematic approach to resolving conflicts and addressing the underlying issues contributing to their anger. By applying problem-solving skills, individuals can identify triggers, communicate their needs effectively, and work collaboratively with others to find solutions that promote understanding, cooperation, and mutual respect.

Physiological arousal is the body's natural response to stress or perceived threats. When faced with triggering events or situations, the body releases stress hormones such as adrenaline and cortisol, leading to increased heart rate, muscle tension, and other physical symptoms associated with the "fight or flight" response.

In the context of anger, heightened physiological arousal can exacerbate feelings of anger, making it more difficult to think clearly and respond constructively to triggering events. Learning to manage physiological arousal is therefore an essential skill for anger management.

Relaxation Techniques

Relaxation techniques are strategies and practices designed to reduce stress, tension, and physiological arousal, promoting a sense of calm and well-being. Some common relaxation techniques that can be helpful for managing anger include:

- Deep Breathing: Deep breathing exercises involve taking slow, deep breaths from the diaphragm, focusing on the sensation of the breath as it enters and leaves the body. Deep breathing can help calm the nervous system, reduce muscle tension, and promote relaxation.

- Progressive Muscle Relaxation (PMR): PMR involves systematically tensing and relaxing different muscle groups in the body, starting from the toes and working up to the head. This technique helps individuals become more aware of muscle tension and learn to release it consciously, promoting relaxation and stress relief.

- Mindfulness Meditation: Mindfulness meditation involves bringing awareness to the present moment, observing thoughts, feelings, and sensations without judgment or attachment. By cultivating mindfulness, individuals can develop greater emotional regulation and resilience in the face of triggering events.

- Visualization: Visualization techniques involve mentally imagining peaceful and calming scenes or experiences, such as a serene beach or a tranquil forest. Visualization can evoke feelings of relaxation and well-being, reducing stress and tension in the body.

Incorporating Relaxation Techniques into Daily Practice

To reap the benefits of relaxation techniques, it's essential to incorporate them into daily practice as part of a regular self-care routine. This may involve setting aside dedicated time each day for relaxation exercises, such as in the morning or before bed, or integrating relaxation techniques into daily activities, such as during breaks at work or before engaging in stressful tasks.

Consistency and persistence are key to mastering relaxation techniques and experiencing their full benefits. Over time, individuals can develop greater awareness of their body's stress response and learn to intervene effectively to promote relaxation and emotional well-being.

Integrating Relaxation Techniques with Other Strategies

Relaxation techniques can be used in conjunction with other behavioral strategies for anger control, such as cognitive restructuring, assertiveness training, and problem-solving skills. By combining relaxation techniques with cognitive and behavioral interventions, individuals can develop a comprehensive toolkit for managing anger and promoting emotional regulation in various situations.

5. Mindfulness and Anger

The Role of Mindfulness in Anger Management

Mindfulness is the practice of bringing focused attention and non-judgmental awareness to the present moment. It involves observing thoughts, feelings, sensations, and external stimuli without attachment or reactivity. Mindfulness encourages individuals to cultivate an attitude of openness, curiosity, and acceptance towards their inner experiences.

Cultivating Self-Awareness

One of the key benefits of mindfulness in anger management is its ability to cultivate self-awareness. By practicing mindfulness, individuals learn to observe their thoughts, feelings, and bodily sensations as they arise in the present moment. This heightened awareness allows individuals to recognize the early signs of anger—such as racing thoughts, increased heart rate, or muscle tension—and intervene before anger escalates out of control.

Developing Emotional Regulation

Mindfulness also plays a crucial role in emotional regulation by providing individuals with tools to respond to anger in a more skillful and adaptive way. Rather than reacting impulsively to triggering events, individuals learn to pause, observe their emotional responses with curiosity and compassion, and choose a response that aligns with their values and intentions.

Cultivating Compassion and Empathy

Another key aspect of mindfulness in anger management is its capacity to cultivate compassion and empathy towards oneself and others. By practicing self-compassion, individuals learn to recognize and validate their own suffering without judgment or self-criticism. This self-compassionate stance allows individuals to respond to anger with kindness and understanding, rather than harshness or blame.

Similarly, mindfulness fosters empathy towards others by encouraging individuals to adopt a non-judgmental and compassionate attitude towards the experiences of others. By recognizing the interconnectedness of all beings and the universal nature of suffering, individuals can respond to anger in others with empathy and understanding, rather than defensiveness or hostility.

Integrating Mindfulness into Daily Life

To reap the benefits of mindfulness in anger management, it's essential to integrate mindfulness into daily life as a regular practice. This may involve setting aside dedicated time each day for formal mindfulness meditation, as well as incorporating informal mindfulness practices into daily activities, such as mindful breathing, eating, or walking.

Consistency and persistence are key to developing a mindfulness practice that supports anger management and emotional well-being. Over time, individuals can cultivate greater self-awareness, emotional regulation, and compassion, empowering them to respond to anger with wisdom and skillfulness in all aspects of their lives.

Mindfulness-Based Cognitive Therapy (MBCT)

MBCT was developed as a relapse prevention intervention for individuals with recurrent depression. It combines elements of cognitive therapy with mindfulness practices derived from mindfulness-based stress reduction (MBSR). The primary goal of MBCT is to help individuals develop greater awareness of their thoughts, feelings, and bodily sensations and to learn to relate to them with acceptance and compassion.

Adapting MBCT for Anger Management

While MBCT was originally designed for depression, its principles and techniques can be adapted and applied to a wide range of emotional difficulties, including anger. By cultivating mindfulness and adopting a non-judgmental stance towards their experiences, individuals can learn to recognize the early signs of anger, interrupt automatic patterns of reactivity, and respond to triggering events with greater clarity and equanimity.

Core Components of MBCT

MBCT typically consists of an 8-week program that includes the following core components:

- Mindfulness Meditation Practices: Participants engage in various mindfulness meditation practices, such as body scan, sitting meditation, and mindful movement. These practices help individuals develop focused attention, cultivate present-moment awareness, and cultivate an attitude of acceptance and non-reactivity towards their experiences.

- Cognitive Restructuring: MBCT incorporates cognitive therapy techniques to help individuals identify and challenge maladaptive thought patterns associated with anger. By examining the accuracy and utility of their thoughts, individuals can develop more balanced and adaptive ways of thinking about triggering events and responding to them.

- Relapse Prevention Strategies: MBCT includes relapse prevention strategies to help individuals anticipate and respond to challenges that may arise in the future. By identifying triggers, early warning signs, and coping strategies, individuals can develop a personalized plan for maintaining their gains and preventing relapse.

Benefits of MBCT for Anger Management

Research has shown that MBCT can be effective in reducing anger and aggression and improving emotional regulation and well-being. By cultivating mindfulness and adopting a non-reactive stance towards their experiences, individuals learn to respond to anger with greater awareness, compassion, and skillfulness, rather than reacting impulsively or habitually.

Integrating MBCT into Anger Management

To integrate MBCT into anger management, individuals can participate in structured MBCT programs offered by trained instructors or therapists. Additionally, individuals can incorporate mindfulness practices into their daily lives as a regular self-care routine, engaging in formal meditation practices and informal mindfulness exercises to cultivate present-moment awareness and emotional resilience.

Practicing Mindfulness: Exercises and Strategies

Mindful Breathing

Mindful breathing is a simple yet powerful mindfulness practice that involves bringing focused attention to the sensations of the breath as it moves in and out of the body. To practice mindful breathing:

- Find a quiet and comfortable place to sit or lie down.
- Close your eyes and bring your attention to your breath.
- Notice the sensations of the breath as it enters and leaves your body.
- If your mind wanders, gently bring your attention back to the breath without judgment or criticism.
- Practice for a few minutes each day, gradually increasing the duration as you become more comfortable with the practice.

Mindful breathing can help individuals cultivate focused attention, calm the nervous system, and reduce physiological arousal associated with anger.

Body Scan Meditation

Body scan meditation is a mindfulness practice that involves systematically scanning the body from head to toe, bringing awareness to sensations, tensions, and areas of discomfort. To practice body scan meditation:

- Find a comfortable lying position and close your eyes.
- Begin by bringing your attention to your breath, allowing yourself to relax and settle into the present moment.
- Starting from the top of your head, slowly scan down through your body, noticing any sensations, tensions, or areas of discomfort.
- As you encounter each sensation, simply observe it with curiosity and acceptance, without trying to change or fix anything.
- Continue scanning down through your body, moving at your own pace, until you reach your toes.
- When you're ready, gently bring your attention back to your breath and gradually transition back to the present moment.

Body scan meditation can help individuals develop greater awareness of bodily sensations, release tension and stress, and cultivate a sense of ease and relaxation.

Mindful Walking

Mindful walking is a mindfulness practice that involves bringing awareness to the sensations of walking, such as the movement of the feet, the shifting of weight, and the contact with the ground. To practice mindful walking:

- Find a quiet and safe place to walk, such as a park or garden.
- Begin by bringing your attention to your feet and the sensations of contact with the ground.
- Slowly begin walking at a comfortable pace, noticing the movement of your feet and legs with each step.
- As you walk, bring your attention to the physical sensations of walking, such as the lifting and lowering of the feet, the shifting of weight from side to side, and the rhythm of the breath.
- If your mind wanders, gently bring your attention back to the sensations of walking without judgment or criticism.
- Continue walking mindfully for a few minutes, allowing yourself to fully immerse in the experience of walking.

Mindful walking can help individuals ground themselves in the present moment, reduce rumination and overthinking, and cultivate a sense of connection with the environment.

Loving-Kindness Meditation

Loving-kindness meditation is a mindfulness practice that involves cultivating feelings of love, compassion, and kindness towards oneself and others. To practice loving-kindness meditation:

- Find a quiet and comfortable place to sit or lie down.

- Close your eyes and bring your attention to your breath, allowing yourself to relax and settle into the present moment.

- Begin by silently repeating phrases of loving-kindness to yourself, such as "May I be happy, may I be healthy, may I be safe, may I live with ease."

- As you repeat these phrases, imagine sending feelings of love, warmth, and kindness towards yourself, bathing yourself in these positive intentions.

- After a few minutes, gradually expand your circle of loving-kindness to include others, such as loved ones, acquaintances, and even difficult people in your life.

- Silently repeat phrases of loving-kindness towards each person, wishing them happiness, health, safety, and ease.

Loving-kindness meditation can help individuals cultivate feelings of compassion and empathy towards themselves and others, promoting emotional resilience and well-being.

Part III: Applying CBT in Everyday Life

6. Managing Anger in Relationships

Communicating Assertively with Loved Ones

Assertive communication is the ability to express one's thoughts, feelings, and needs openly, honestly, and respectfully, while also respecting the rights and boundaries of others. In the context of relationships, assertive communication is crucial for addressing conflicts, resolving disagreements, and fostering mutual understanding and respect.

Unlike passive communication, which involves avoiding conflict and suppressing one's needs and feelings, or aggressive communication, which involves asserting one's needs at the expense of others' rights and feelings, assertive communication seeks to find a balance between expressing oneself and respecting others.

Strategies for Communicating Assertively with Loved Ones

When expressing anger or addressing conflicts with loved ones, it's important to approach the conversation with intention, empathy, and respect. Some practical strategies for communicating assertively with loved ones include:

- Choose the Right Time and Place: Pick a time and place where both parties can engage in the conversation calmly and without distractions. Avoid discussing sensitive topics when either party is tired, stressed, or preoccupied.

- Use "I" Statements: Frame your thoughts, feelings, and needs using "I" statements to take ownership of your experiences and avoid blaming or accusing the other person. For example, instead of saying, "You always make me angry," try saying, "I feel frustrated when..."

- Practice Active Listening: Listen attentively to the other person's perspective without interrupting or judging. Reflect back what you hear to ensure mutual understanding and demonstrate empathy and respect.

- Express Empathy and Understanding: Acknowledge the other person's feelings and perspective, even if you disagree with them. Validate their experiences and demonstrate empathy and understanding.

- Focus on Solutions, Not Blame: Shift the focus of the conversation from assigning blame to finding mutually acceptable solutions to the underlying issues or conflicts. Collaborate with the other person to brainstorm potential solutions and work together towards resolution.

Setting Boundaries

In addition to communicating assertively, it's important to establish and maintain healthy boundaries in relationships. Boundaries help individuals define their personal limits, protect their emotional well-being, and maintain autonomy and self-respect.

When setting boundaries, it's important to communicate them clearly and assertively with loved ones, expressing your needs and preferences while also respecting the rights and boundaries of others. Be firm and consistent in enforcing your boundaries, and be prepared to assertively assert them when necessary.

Conflict Resolution Skills for Couples

Conflict arises when individuals have differing needs, preferences, or perspectives, leading to tension, disagreement, and sometimes anger. In relationships, conflicts can stem from various sources, including communication breakdowns, unmet expectations, and differences in values or priorities.

It's important for couples to recognize that conflict is a natural and normal part of any relationship and that how they respond to conflict can either strengthen or weaken their bond.

Effective Conflict Resolution Strategies

Effective conflict resolution involves a collaborative and respectful approach to addressing disagreements and finding mutually acceptable solutions. Some key conflict resolution strategies for couples include:

- Active Listening: Each partner should practice active listening, attentively and empathetically listening to the other's perspective without interrupting or judging. Reflecting back what you hear can help ensure mutual understanding and demonstrate empathy.
- Using "I" Statements: When expressing concerns or grievances, use "I" statements to express your thoughts, feelings, and needs without blaming or accusing the other person. For example, instead of saying, "You never listen to me," try saying, "I feel unheard when..."
- Seeking Compromise: Conflict resolution often involves finding compromises that honor both partners' needs and preferences. Each partner

should be willing to give and take, prioritizing the health and happiness of the relationship over being "right" or winning the argument.

- Taking Time-Outs: When emotions run high, it can be helpful to take a time-out to cool down and collect your thoughts before continuing the discussion. Agree on a signal or phrase that indicates the need for a time-out, and set a time to reconvene when both partners are calmer and more receptive.

- Focusing on Solutions: Instead of dwelling on past grievances or assigning blame, focus on finding solutions to the current issue at hand. Brainstorm together and explore different options until you find a solution that feels acceptable to both partners.

Navigating Anger in Conflict

Anger is a common emotion that arises during conflicts, but it's important for couples to navigate anger constructively and respectfully. Some strategies for managing anger in conflict include:

- Taking Responsibility for Emotions: Each partner should take responsibility for their own emotions and reactions, recognizing that they are responsible for how they express and manage their anger.

- Expressing Anger Appropriately: It's okay to feel angry, but it's not okay to express anger in harmful or destructive ways. Find healthy and constructive ways to express anger, such as using assertive communication, taking a time-out, or engaging in physical activity to release tension.

Cultivating Emotional Intimacy

Conflict resolution isn't just about resolving disagreements; it's also an opportunity for couples to deepen their emotional connection and intimacy. By navigating conflicts with honesty, empathy, and respect, couples can build trust, strengthen their bond, and foster a deeper understanding of each other's needs and perspectives.

Building Healthy Boundaries

Boundaries are the invisible lines that define the limits and expectations within a relationship. They encompass physical, emotional, and psychological boundaries that individuals set to protect their autonomy, values, and well-being. Healthy boundaries help individuals maintain a sense of self-respect, autonomy, and integrity while fostering mutual respect and understanding in relationships.

Types of Boundaries

There are several types of boundaries that individuals can establish in relationships:

- Physical Boundaries: Physical boundaries involve respecting each other's personal space, privacy, and physical comfort levels. This includes respecting each other's physical boundaries, such as personal space, touch, and affection.

- Emotional Boundaries: Emotional boundaries involve recognizing and respecting each other's emotional needs, feelings, and experiences. This includes setting limits on sharing personal information, respecting confidentiality, and supporting each other's emotional well-being without taking on each other's emotional burdens.

- Time Boundaries: Time boundaries involve respecting each other's time, commitments, and priorities. This includes setting aside dedicated time for each other, respecting each other's schedules, and balancing individual and shared activities and responsibilities.

- Communication Boundaries: Communication boundaries involve respecting each other's communication preferences, styles, and boundaries.

This includes setting limits on topics of conversation, respecting each other's need for space or time alone, and communicating assertively and respectfully.

Establishing Healthy Boundaries

Establishing healthy boundaries requires clear communication, self-awareness, and mutual respect. Some strategies for establishing healthy boundaries in relationships include:

- Self-Reflection: Take time to reflect on your own needs, values, and boundaries, and communicate them openly and assertively with your partner. Be clear and specific about what you are comfortable with and what you are not.
- Open Communication: Foster open and honest communication with your partner, where both parties feel comfortable expressing their needs, concerns, and boundaries without fear of judgment or criticism. Listen actively and empathetically to your partner's perspective and be willing to negotiate and compromise when necessary.
- Consistency: Be consistent in enforcing your boundaries and following through with consequences when they are violated. This helps

reinforce your boundaries and communicates to your partner that you take them seriously.

- Respect Each Other's Boundaries: Respect your partner's boundaries and expect the same in return. Avoid pressuring or manipulating your partner into crossing their boundaries and be mindful of their comfort levels and limits.

Maintaining Healthy Boundaries

Maintaining healthy boundaries requires ongoing communication, self-awareness, and mutual respect. Some strategies for maintaining healthy boundaries in relationships include:

- Regular Check-Ins: Regularly check in with your partner to assess the status of your boundaries and address any concerns or issues that may arise. Be open to revisiting and adjusting your boundaries as needed to accommodate changing circumstances or needs.

- Self-Care: Prioritize self-care and self-awareness, taking time to nurture your own needs, interests, and well-being. Remember that setting and maintaining healthy boundaries is an act of self-respect and self-care.

- **Seek Support:** If you're struggling to establish or maintain healthy boundaries in your relationship, consider seeking support from a couples therapist or counselor who can provide guidance and tools for navigating boundary issues and fostering a healthier dynamic.

7. Anger in the Workplace

Anger in the workplace can manifest in different forms, including:

- Verbal Outbursts: Yelling, shouting, or using aggressive language towards colleagues or superiors.

- Passive-Aggressive Behavior: Indirect expressions of anger, such as sarcasm, gossip, or withholding information or cooperation.

- Physical Signs: Physical signs of anger, such as clenched fists, flushed face, or tense body language.

- Emotional Withdrawal: Withdrawing from interactions, avoiding communication, or isolating oneself from colleagues.

Recognizing these signs is essential for addressing anger in the workplace before it escalates into more significant conflicts or disruptions.

Strategies for Managing Anger in the Workplace

Managing anger in professional settings requires a combination of self-awareness, emotional regulation, and effective communication. Some strategies for dealing with anger in the workplace include:

- Take a Pause: When faced with a triggering situation, take a moment to pause and collect your thoughts before reacting impulsively. Use deep breathing or visualization techniques to calm yourself down and regain perspective.

- Express Yourself Assertively: If you need to address a source of frustration or conflict, do so assertively and respectfully. Use "I" statements to express your concerns and focus on finding constructive solutions rather than assigning blame.

- Practice Empathy: Cultivate empathy towards your colleagues and seek to understand their perspectives and experiences. Recognize that everyone has their own stressors and challenges, and try to approach conflicts with compassion and understanding.

- Set Boundaries: Establish clear boundaries around acceptable behavior in the workplace and communicate them openly with your colleagues. Respect others' boundaries and expect the same in return, creating a more respectful and harmonious work environment.

Conflict Resolution Skills

Conflict is a natural part of any workplace, but it's essential to address conflicts constructively and respectfully. Some conflict resolution skills that can help manage anger in professional settings include:

- Active Listening: Listen attentively to your colleagues' perspectives and concerns without interrupting or judging. Reflect back what you hear to ensure mutual understanding and demonstrate empathy.
- Seek Common Ground: Focus on areas of agreement and common goals when addressing conflicts, rather than dwelling on differences or past grievances. Collaborate with your colleagues to find mutually acceptable solutions to the issue at hand.
- Stay Professional: Maintain a professional demeanor and tone when addressing conflicts or disagreements in the workplace. Avoid personal attacks or disrespectful behavior, and focus on finding solutions that benefit the team as a whole.

Creating a Positive Work Environment

Ultimately, creating a positive work environment is essential for managing anger and fostering healthy relationships among colleagues. Some strategies for creating a positive work environment include:

- Promote Open Communication: Encourage open and honest communication among colleagues, where everyone feels comfortable expressing their thoughts, concerns, and ideas without fear of judgment or reprisal.

- Recognize Achievements: Acknowledge and celebrate the achievements and contributions of your colleagues, fostering a sense of appreciation and camaraderie in the workplace.

- Provide Support: Offer support and assistance to your colleagues when needed, whether it's through lending a listening ear, providing guidance, or helping out with tasks or projects.

- Lead by Example: Lead by example by demonstrating professionalism, respect, and empathy in your interactions with colleagues. Your behavior sets the tone for the work environment and can influence the behavior of others.

Assertive communication is the ability to express one's thoughts, feelings, and needs in a clear, honest, and respectful manner while also respecting the rights and boundaries of others. Unlike passive communication, which involves avoiding conflict and suppressing one's needs, or aggressive communication, which involves asserting one's needs at the expense of others, assertive communication seeks to find a balance between expressing oneself and respecting others.

Strategies for Assertive Communication with Colleagues

When communicating assertively with colleagues, it's essential to approach the conversation with professionalism, empathy, and respect. Some strategies for assertive communication with colleagues include:

- Choose the Right Time and Place: Pick a time and place where both parties can engage in the conversation calmly and without distractions. Avoid discussing sensitive topics in front of others or in high-stress environments.
- Be Clear and Specific: Clearly and specifically express your thoughts, feelings, and needs using "I"

statements. Avoid making assumptions or generalizations, and focus on providing concrete examples to illustrate your point.

- Listen Actively: Listen attentively to your colleague's perspective without interrupting or judging. Reflect back what you hear to ensure mutual understanding and demonstrate empathy and respect.

- Seek Solutions, Not Blame: Shift the focus of the conversation from assigning blame to finding mutually acceptable solutions to the issue at hand. Collaborate with your colleague to brainstorm potential solutions and work together towards resolution.

Strategies for Assertive Communication with Supervisors

Communicating assertively with supervisors requires professionalism, tact, and diplomacy. Some strategies for assertive communication with supervisors include:

- Prepare in Advance: Before approaching your supervisor with a concern or request, take time to prepare your thoughts and plan your approach. Anticipate potential questions or objections and be ready to address them.

- Focus on Solutions: When addressing issues with your supervisor, focus on finding solutions rather than dwelling on problems. Offer constructive suggestions or alternatives and be prepared to collaborate on finding a resolution.

- Be Respectful and Professional: Maintain a respectful and professional demeanor when communicating with your supervisor, even if you're addressing a sensitive or challenging topic. Avoid becoming defensive or confrontational, and instead, focus on maintaining open and honest communication.

- Follow Up: After the conversation, follow up with your supervisor to ensure that any agreements or decisions are implemented effectively. Express gratitude for their time and attention, and be willing to continue the dialogue as needed.

Overcoming Challenges

Assertive communication can be challenging, especially in high-stakes or emotionally charged situations. Some common challenges to assertive communication in the workplace include fear of confrontation, lack of confidence, and cultural or organizational barriers.

To overcome these challenges, it's essential to practice self-awareness, self-compassion, and resilience. Take small steps to assert yourself gradually, starting with low-risk situations and gradually building confidence over time. Seek support from trusted colleagues, mentors, or professional development resources to build your assertiveness skills and overcome obstacles.

Stress Management Techniques for Work-Related Anger

Work-related anger can stem from a variety of sources, including:

- High workload and tight deadlines
- Interpersonal conflicts with colleagues or supervisors
- Micromanagement or lack of autonomy
- Feeling undervalued or unappreciated
- Organizational changes or restructuring
- Discrimination or unfair treatment

Recognizing the sources of work-related anger is the first step towards effectively managing it.

Stress Management Techniques

Effective stress management can help individuals cope with work-related anger and prevent it from escalating into more significant issues. Here are some stress management techniques specifically tailored for the workplace:

- Time Management: Prioritize tasks and deadlines to ensure that workloads are manageable and deadlines are met. Break larger tasks into smaller, more manageable steps, and delegate tasks when possible.

- Mindfulness Meditation: Take short breaks throughout the day to practice mindfulness meditation. Focus on your breath or engage in a brief body scan to bring awareness to your thoughts, feelings, and bodily sensations. Mindfulness can help reduce stress and promote emotional regulation.

- Physical Exercise: Incorporate regular physical exercise into your routine, such as walking, jogging, or yoga. Exercise helps release tension and stress hormones, promoting relaxation and improving mood.

- Stress-Relief Techniques: Practice stress-relief techniques such as deep breathing exercises, progressive muscle relaxation, or visualization. These techniques can help reduce muscle tension, lower blood pressure, and promote a sense of calm.

- Setting Boundaries: Establish clear boundaries around work hours, workload, and availability. Learn to say no to additional tasks or commitments when necessary, and prioritize self-care and work-life balance.

Coping with Interpersonal Conflicts

Interpersonal conflicts in the workplace can contribute to feelings of anger and stress. Here are some strategies for coping with and resolving interpersonal conflicts:

- Active Listening: Listen attentively to the other person's perspective without interrupting or judging. Reflect back what you hear to ensure mutual understanding and demonstrate empathy.

- Seeking Mediation: If conflicts persist, consider seeking mediation from a neutral third party, such as a supervisor or HR professional. Mediation can help facilitate constructive dialogue and find mutually acceptable solutions.

- Conflict Resolution Skills: Practice conflict resolution skills such as assertive communication, problem-solving, and compromise. Focus on finding solutions to the underlying issues rather than dwelling on blame or grievances.

Creating a Supportive Work Environment

Building a supportive work environment can help reduce work-related stress and promote emotional well-being. Here are some strategies for creating a supportive work environment:

- Promote Open Communication: Encourage open and honest communication among colleagues and supervisors. Create opportunities for feedback, discussion, and collaboration.

- Recognize and Reward: Acknowledge and reward employees for their contributions and achievements. Recognize their efforts and celebrate successes, fostering a sense of appreciation and morale.

- Provide Resources: Offer resources and support for stress management, such as employee assistance programs, mental health resources, and wellness initiatives.

8. Self-Care and Long-Term Anger Management

Developing a Personalized Anger Management Plan

Developing a Personalized Anger Management Plan

Anger management is not just about dealing with anger in the moment; it's also about developing long-term strategies for managing anger and promoting emotional well-being.

Assessing Your Anger Triggers and Patterns

The first step in developing a personalized anger management plan is to identify your unique anger triggers and patterns. Take some time to reflect on past experiences of anger and consider the following questions:

- What situations or circumstances tend to trigger your anger?

- How do you typically respond when you feel angry?

- Are there any recurring patterns or themes in your anger triggers?

- How does anger affect your thoughts, feelings, and behaviors?

By gaining insight into your anger triggers and patterns, you can begin to develop strategies for managing anger more effectively.

Identifying Coping Strategies and Resources

Once you've identified your anger triggers and patterns, it's essential to explore coping strategies and resources that can help you manage anger more effectively. Consider the following approaches:

- Cognitive-Behavioral Techniques: Cognitive-behavioral techniques, such as cognitive restructuring and problem-solving skills, can help you challenge and change negative thought patterns and behaviors that contribute to anger.
- Mindfulness and Relaxation Techniques: Practicing mindfulness meditation, deep breathing exercises, or progressive muscle relaxation can help reduce stress and promote emotional regulation, making it easier to manage anger in the moment.
- Healthy Lifestyle Habits: Prioritize self-care by adopting healthy lifestyle habits, such as regular exercise, nutritious eating, adequate sleep, and stress management techniques. Taking care of your physical and emotional well-being can help reduce overall stress levels and improve mood.

- Social Support Networks: Build a support network of friends, family members, or support groups who can offer encouragement, understanding, and practical assistance during times of stress or anger.

Creating an Action Plan

Based on your assessment of anger triggers and coping strategies, create a personalized action plan for managing anger more effectively. Your action plan might include:

- Identifying Warning Signs: Recognize early warning signs of anger, such as physical tension, racing thoughts, or irritability, and take proactive steps to intervene before anger escalates.

- Implementing Coping Strategies: Practice coping strategies such as deep breathing, mindfulness meditation, or assertive communication when you feel anger arising. Experiment with different techniques to find what works best for you.

Reviewing and Adjusting Your Plan

Regularly review and evaluate your anger management plan to assess its effectiveness and make any necessary adjustments. Keep track of your progress, noting any improvements or challenges you encounter along the way. Be open to revisiting and revising your plan as needed to ensure it remains relevant and supportive of your long-term goals.

Lifestyle Changes for Anger Reduction

In addition to specific coping strategies, lifestyle changes can play a crucial role in long-term anger management. This section will delve into various lifestyle adjustments that can contribute to reducing anger and promoting emotional well-being over time.

Prioritize Physical Activity

Regular exercise is one of the most effective ways to manage stress and reduce anger. Engaging in physical activity releases endorphins, the body's natural mood lifters, which can help alleviate feelings of anger and frustration. Aim for at least 30 minutes of moderate-intensity exercise most days of the week. This can include activities such as walking, jogging, swimming, yoga, or cycling. Find an activity you enjoy and make it a regular part of your routine.

Practice Stress Management Techniques

Chronic stress can exacerbate feelings of anger and contribute to its escalation. Incorporating stress management techniques into your daily life can help mitigate its effects and reduce anger. Techniques such as deep breathing exercises, progressive muscle relaxation, mindfulness meditation, and visualization can all help promote relaxation and emotional balance. Experiment with different techniques to find what works best for you, and make them a regular part of your self-care routine.

Improve Sleep Quality

Lack of sleep can significantly impact mood regulation and increase irritability and anger. Prioritize getting adequate sleep each night to support emotional well-being. Aim for 7-9 hours of quality sleep by establishing a regular sleep schedule, creating a relaxing bedtime routine, and creating a comfortable sleep environment free from distractions. Avoid caffeine, electronic devices, and stimulating activities close to bedtime, as these can interfere with sleep quality.

Adopt a Healthy Diet

Nutrition plays a significant role in overall well-being, including emotional health. Eating a balanced diet rich in fruits, vegetables, whole grains, lean proteins, and healthy fats can provide essential nutrients that support mood regulation and reduce anger. Limit consumption of processed foods, sugary snacks, and excessive caffeine, as these can contribute to mood swings and irritability. Stay hydrated by drinking plenty of water throughout the day, as even mild dehydration can impact mood and cognitive function.

Cultivate Supportive Relationships

Healthy relationships can provide valuable support and encouragement, helping to buffer against stress and anger. Cultivate supportive relationships with friends, family members, or peers who can offer empathy, understanding, and perspective during challenging times. Make time for meaningful social connections and prioritize spending quality time with loved ones. Communicate openly and honestly with trusted individuals about your feelings and experiences, and seek their support when needed.

Manage Time Effectively

Feeling overwhelmed by a busy schedule or excessive demands can contribute to stress and anger. Manage your time effectively by prioritizing tasks, setting realistic goals, and practicing time management techniques such as breaking tasks into smaller steps, delegating responsibilities when possible, and setting boundaries around work and personal time. Avoid overcommitting yourself and learn to say no to additional obligations when necessary to protect your well-being.

Individual therapy, particularly cognitive-behavioral therapy (CBT), is a highly effective approach for managing anger. In therapy, you can work with a trained therapist to explore the underlying causes of your anger, identify maladaptive thought patterns and behaviors, and develop practical strategies for coping with anger in healthier ways.

- Cognitive Restructuring: Therapists use cognitive restructuring techniques to help you challenge and reframe negative thought patterns that contribute to anger. By identifying and disputing irrational beliefs, you can develop more balanced and realistic perspectives on challenging situations.

- Behavioral Techniques: Therapists may also teach you behavioral techniques, such as relaxation exercises, assertiveness training, and problem-solving skills, to help you manage anger more effectively in real-life situations. Through role-playing and behavioral experiments, you can practice new skills and build confidence in your ability to handle anger-provoking situations.

- Emotion Regulation: Therapy can help you develop emotion regulation skills to better understand and manage your feelings of anger. By learning to identify and label your emotions, tolerate distress, and engage in healthy coping strategies, you can reduce the intensity and frequency of angry outbursts.

Support Groups for Anger Management

Joining a support group for anger management can provide valuable peer support, encouragement, and accountability. In a supportive group setting, you can share your experiences, learn from others facing similar challenges, and receive validation and feedback from peers who understand what you're going through.

- Mutual Support: Support groups offer a sense of camaraderie and understanding, as members share their struggles, successes, and coping strategies related to anger management. Knowing that you're not alone in your experiences can be incredibly validating and empowering.

- Learning from Others: Hearing others' stories and perspectives can provide valuable insight and inspiration for your own journey towards anger management. You may discover new coping strategies, perspectives, or resources that you hadn't considered before.

- Accountability: Support groups provide a supportive environment for setting and achieving goals related to anger management. Knowing that you'll be reporting back to the group can provide added motivation and accountability to stick with your self-care practices and coping strategies.

Online Resources for Anger Management

In addition to therapy and support groups, there are numerous online resources available for anger management, including websites, forums, articles, and self-help books. Online resources can provide information, guidance, and practical tools for managing anger, even if you're unable to access in-person support.

- Educational Resources: Websites and articles offer educational resources on anger management, including information on common triggers, coping strategies, and relaxation techniques. You can learn about the psychological and physiological aspects of anger and explore evidence-based approaches for managing it.

- Self-Help Tools: Many online resources offer self-help tools and exercises for managing anger, such as downloadable worksheets, guided meditations, and interactive quizzes. These tools can help you deepen your understanding of anger and develop practical skills for managing it more effectively.

- Community Support: Online forums and social media groups provide opportunities to connect with others facing similar challenges with anger management. Engaging with an online community can offer support, validation, and encouragement, even from the comfort of your own home.

Conclusion

Embracing a Life Free from Unnecessary Anger

In the journey of embracing a life free from unnecessary anger, we've explored the transformative process of letting go of destructive emotions and cultivating a mindset of peace, positivity, and emotional well-being. Recognizing the cost of anger and choosing to let go of it as a default response sets the foundation for change. By cultivating emotional awareness, empathy, and understanding, we can navigate conflicts with grace and compassion.

Forgiveness and gratitude become powerful tools for releasing resentment and cultivating positivity in our lives. Setting boundaries and prioritizing self-care protect our emotional well-being, while commitment to lifelong growth and learning ensures that we continue to evolve and thrive.

Embracing a life free from unnecessary anger is not merely about controlling emotions; it's about embracing a new way of being. It's about choosing empathy over hostility, forgiveness over resentment, and gratitude over bitterness. It's about creating a life filled with peace, purpose, and fulfillment.

As we conclude this discussion, let us remember that change is a journey, and each step forward, no matter how small, brings us closer to the life we envision. Let us continue to cultivate compassion, understanding, and positivity in ourselves and others, and may we always embrace the opportunity to live a life free from unnecessary anger.